From Whence They Came

*From foreign country or neighboring town
they settled in the valley and changed
a ghost town[1] into a community.*

**The Early History of Sunland, California
Volume 8**

ML Tiernan

From Whence They Came

www.maryleetiernan.com
Second printing April 1, 2015
10 9 8 7 6 5 4 3 2

ISBN 978-0983067276 (Paperback)

©2001 ©2010 Mary Lee Tiernan. All rights reserved. No portion of this product may be photographed, scanned, translated, reproduced, copied, or reduced to any tangible or electronic medium or machine-readable form, without the prior written consent of Mary Lee Tiernan.

Photograph on cover courtesy of A. Elizabeth Schell. Quote on cover from "Sunland First Developed in Big 1887 Land Boom."

Contents

Coming to Sunland 5

The Next Generation 13

Map of Sunland Families 27

Footnotes 28

Bibliography 30

The Early History of Sunland, California series 32

Author's Notes

The researcher, like a detective, examines the evidence to try to determine the real story. Unfortunately for researchers, we cannot re-examine witnesses or revisit scenes because in most cases, they have long since disappeared. So we sort through the conflicting data to find the most reliable and logical explanations. I have done my best to follow the clues and weave as authentic a story as possible.

My thanks to the staff at Bolton Hall Museum, Tujunga, California, for their assistance with this project.

Coming to Sunland

After the great Land Boom of the 1880s[2] ended, settlers continued to migrate to California, not for gold, but for oranges and warm weather. The famous Pasadena Tournament of Roses began in 1890 as part of the new strategy to promote Southern California. And what could

William and Amelia Adams Blumfield.
Photos courtesy of A. Elizabeth Schell.

advertise the temperate climate better than staging an outdoor parade with fresh flowers in the middle of winter? Many of these new civic-minded pioneers had the means to improve the lands they bought. Settlers of moderate means tended to migrate to the country areas outside Los Angeles.

Amelia Blumfield[3] wasn't thinking about oranges or warm weather or even gold; she just plain missed her family. Years earlier, in 1873, Amelia, her husband William[4], and their four children had left England and migrated to Canada to join some of her twelve brothers and sisters. They'd managed all right in Canada: William working as a carpenter, she as a midwife. She'd earned about $2.40 a week caring for newborns and their mothers.

But by 1894, her brothers[5] and sister, and even one daughter, had moved on to California, and she missed them. When news of the birth of her grandson[6] in Pasadena arrived, that, and the lure of the low $12 railroad rates to California, seemed good enough reasons to pack up her family and their possessions once more. Out came the pine trunk William had made for their trip to Canada.[7]

Like many who came to California to visit, Amelia and William decided to stay. They bought twenty acres of land, dotted with clusters of oak trees, in the small community of Sunland, where her youngest brother Alfred Adams lived. The village, which only had one store[8], had been renamed Sunland in 1887 because the postal officials refused to accept the name Monte Vista. The town of "Monta" Vista already existed, and they decided the similar spellings of "Monta" and "Monte" would cause confusion. Why the name Sunland? M.V. Hartranft, a land developer in the early 1900s wrote in a sales brochure: "They (Verdugo Mountains) roll back the fog banks from the sea, much as you would raise a curtain to let the sunshine in—and the early settlers called it Sunland. Which it is."[9]

The Blumfield land, adjacent to the center of town, stretched from Hillrose Street north to Wentworth Street

Amelia and William's first home under the oaks. Picture dates prior to 1905. Photo courtesy of A. Elizabeth Schell.

and from Sherman Grove Avenue east approximately 600feet. With plenty of wood available, William set to work using his carpentry skills and built a house on Hillrose in the shade of the oak trees.[10]

Amelia watched eagerly as William erected their two-story home. She envisioned the many hours they would relax in their easy chairs looking out the bay window in the living room. When company came, the spacious room accommodated a large dining table, although they tended to eat most meals in the kitchen. In addition to a bedroom, a special room also shared the ground floor space, for William planned built-in luxuries for Amelia's new house. Her kitchen featured a sink with running water, and the special room housed a wood-framed bathtub lined with metal.

Under the stairs to the two upstairs rooms, William built a pantry. Years later Amelia's grandchildren would remember her taking homemade bread from that pantry and, holding it against herself, cut off a slice. After spreading it with home-churned butter, she sprinkled sugar on top as a treat.

Amelia lovingly cared for her new home. To clean the bare pine wood floors, she took damp tea leaves from the ever-present tea pot and sprinkled them on the floor to keep the dust down while she swept.

Besides building their home and doing other paid carpentry jobs, William worked in the local olive groves until he could clear his own land. Slowly, with help from relatives and neighbors[11], the Blumfields prepared the land and planted it with apricot and peach trees, and later grape vines. A 500 gallon tank in the backyard stored water from Big Tujunga Canyon which they pumped into the orchard.

Early Sunland farmers depended on water from Big Tujunga Canyon to irrigate the dry land. They formed a cooperative, the Mutual Water Company, and built irrigation ditches to carry the water to their groves. The company charged either time or money for the amount of

Elizabeth and Russ on their little red chairs.
Photo courtesy of A. Elizabeth Schell.

water each member used on a monthly basis. Money bought needed materials. Time meant working on the line and making repairs, a never-ending project given the poor condition of the pipes and the constant breakage. The flume through the Blumfield orchards ran east from Sherman Grove, then curved around heading south to Hillrose Street. Its path approximates Forsythe Street.

Behind the house stood a barn with horse stalls and a shed for hay where Amelia raised turkeys. They proved to be challenging and difficult to raise. Their son Alfred worked alongside William for twelve years, clearing and planting the land and tending the orchard until his marriage in 1906. When he married, Amelia and William gave Alfred and his wife one acre of land on Sherman Grove as a wedding present. Amelia's grandchildren arrived shortly thereafter.

The grandchildren, Russ and Elizabeth, loved to visit their grandparents. They would drag their little red chairs almost daily over the sandy path between their house and their grandparents'. Amelia always welcomed them with the door opened wide. Should they arrive at mealtime, they seated themselves on their red chairs while Grandfather said a blessing. Believing children should not drink the strong tea that the adults did, Grandmother served them a special 'tea,' a mixture of hot water and milk, which they hated. The children dragged the chairs back and forth so often that the sandy path ground the ends of the legs down to points.

The site of Amelia's first home in Sunland, however, was not well-chosen. During the winter, the shade from the oaks proved too much for the iron wood-heating stove. If the cold winters weren't enough, the threat of the mighty oaks was. Twenty-nine years earlier, when William had built the house, he laid the foundation among the trees. In 1894, enough room lay between the house and the trees to permit passage in-between, but by 1923, after years of growth, the oaks threatened to brush aside man's feebler structure and claim the ground for itself. Amelia's beloved home was torn down and the lumber used to build a new home in a sunnier location. It was still on Hillrose, but closer to Sherman Grove Avenue.

During the early years of Hollywood, producers often chose the rustic scenery of Sunland, especially Sunland Park and Lancasters Lake, for set locations. The children—all the local kids as well as Russ and Elizabeth—loved climbing around the sets and watching the shoots. Many remember a kind actor or actress who took the time to entertain them. One cowboy, after galloping up and down the hills, stopped and swung Elizabeth up on the saddle for a ride on his horse. Or those movie-making days might even have given them their own special moment on the silver screen. In Mary Pickford's film *Heart of the Hills*, a local boy named Jack James was chosen to fight with Mary in a scene where, as the new girl in school, the kids were making fun of her and she fights back. The 'school' was actually the old church in the park. Many of the children appeared as extras in various films; Elizabeth once received 50¢ to appear in a crowd.

Adults also shared a moment of 'fame and glory' as extras, for which they received as much as $5.00 a day and a box lunch. One script called for a scene of early days and Grandmother Amelia fit the bill perfectly with her hair piled in a bun and her high-necked dresses, which always hung a little longer than the current style. After her debut on the silver screen, she good-naturedly accepted teasing for participating—she who had denounced moving pictures and playing cards as sinful.

Amelia and William celebrated 60 years of marriage before William's death in 1927. Through all those years together, they retained a faint trace of the accent they brought with them from England. Amelia died shortly before her 95th birthday in 1940. She deeded five acres of her property to her daughter Amelia Blumfield (Millie) Tench, and the remaining 14 acres to her son Alfred. The property has since been subdivided for houses. But before that happened, the next generation had its story to tell.

The Next Generation

At the Roscoe depot, a young woman climbed down from the train which paused just long enough to unload the mail and one passenger—herself. The fresh, clean air revived her after the long ride in the stuffy train car. Then she remembered her purpose in coming and her hands shook slightly. A properly dressed gentleman approached, introduced himself as Mr. Rowley, one of the school trustees, and escorted her to a horse and buggy.

They bumped up the hillside on a dirt road, jack rabbits scurrying out of their way. When they finally reached the crest of Watson's Hill[12], she gasped at the beauty of the valley lying before her. But as the distance closed between them and the little village of Sunland, her stomach began to tighten.

After graduating from ninth grade and then the Normal School in Los Angeles, a training institute for teachers, Clara Freeman[13] had come all the way from Downey to apply for a teaching position. The distance may not have been quite as far as her parents had traveled. Her

Clara and Alfred Blumfield on their wedding day in 1906.
Photo courtesy of A. Elizabeth Schell.

father's family originally came from Cape Cod, Massachusetts to Nebraska, and then years later her parents migrated to California. But in those days, for a young woman striking out on her own, it was quite an adventure.

Mr. Rowley drove past the one-room schoolhouse in the northeast corner of Sunland Park—which was about half its current size. It would be many years yet before William Bernhard, another original settler, would donate a parcel of his land to enlarge the park. Clara's knees trembled at the sight of the school and the thought of the impending interview with the other members of the board.

Finally the moment arrived when they stopped in front of the home of Alfred Adams Jr. whose eight children would keep the schoolroom filled for many years. Clara recounted her training and experience, answered their questions, and soon found herself back in the buggy for the four-and-a-half mile ride back to the train. Several days later an offer arrived, and Clara once more boarded the train for Sunland.

During that first year of teaching in 1904, Clara boarded with the Alfred Adams Sr. family and walked three blocks to the one-room school in Sunland Park.[14] Although the exact number of students in Clara's class is unknown, attendance during this period varied from an average of 12 to a high of 20. Transients, attracted by the valley's climate, came and camped for six months to a year at a time. The attendance, or not, of their children caused the fluctuation in enrollment. Sometimes two or three students would be in the same grade level; other times, none. Clara taught all eight grade levels.[15]

Also during her first year, Alfred Tunstill Blumfield[16], another one of the trustees, began courting Clara by never missing the opportunity to drive her back and forth to the Roscoe depot for trips home to visit her family in Downey. During Clara's second year of teaching, she lived with

Clara and Alfred's home at 10738 Sherman Grove Avenue.
Photo courtesy of their daughter A. Elizabeth Schell.

Captain and Mrs. Cushman. Her romance with Alfred blossomed and they decided to marry; Clara was 23, Alfred 27. For their wedding in June 1906, the Cushmans returned Clara's final month's room and board as a wedding present. With this money, the couple bought a piano, which their descendants still use. Alfred's parents, William and Amelia, deeded one of their 20 acres to them. After their honeymoon in Catalina, the couple returned to their new home, built on that acre by Alfred's father and Clara's father, Charles Russell Freeman. Clara and Alfred would spend the next fifty years there, at 10738 Sherman Grove Avenue. The house still stands, as of this writing in

In 2001, the Blumfield house still stood as one of the few structures left from Sunland's earliest days, but not in the best condition.

2001, although in rather deplorable condition.

After her marriage, Clara gave up her teaching position. Alfred and Clara's two children arrived in quick succession: William Russell (Russ) in 1907 and Elizabeth in 1908.[17] Fortunately, instead of a midwife, Clara found a doctor living in the Monte Vista Hotel who delivered both her children in her home on Sherman Grove. Unfortunately, the doctor was from out-of-state and had no California license. Consequently, he failed to report and register the births of her children, leaving them both without birth certificates. In later years, they had some difficulty officially proving that they existed.

For the next twenty-five years or so, Alfred cared for the Wright's olive groves as his primary employment. Although Mr. Wright owned the land stretching north to Hillrose and south to Foothill Boulevard, between McVine on the east and Woodward on the west, he did not live in the valley and left the care of his groves and the harvesting of the olives in the fall in Alfred's capable hands.

Alfred's work necessitated frequent trips to Los Angeles, where he often did the family shopping. Because only about fifty families lived in all of Sunland and Tujunga, few stores existed in the village. When Clara wanted to do her own shopping, she brought the children all the way to Downey on the train to their other set of grandparents and then back again. The long trip with young children meant that it didn't happen too often.

A strong work ethic challenged American settlers, or they would not have accomplished what they did. They continually sought new opportunities to assure a better living for their families and passed that ethic on to their children. As Russ remembers, "My dad always said, 'You can do jobs for me,' so I had to cultivate and hoe. I made

Irene Lancaster, a neighbor, with the Blumfield home in the background. Irene died at age 21 in the 1918-1919 flu pandemic that claimed over 20 million lives. Photo courtesy of Marshall Murray.

my money for my clothes and stuff for school the next year. It helped out—which you had to do in those days."[18]

So in addition to Alfred's steady job working the Wright olive groves, the young couple also helped with William's orchard. After bringing home part of the day's harvest, Alfred and Clara sorted the fruit at night under the huge live oak in the backyard and packed the best fruit for market. The next day, the fruit would be hauled to Los Angeles wholesale sheds. The arrival of electricity around 1913 helped ease the annual sorting task. A long cord from the house to the yard provided light for the night ritual.

During World War I, Alfred rented vineyards from the McVine family, and Clara and the kids spent long days in the vineyards helping to pick grapes. Income from the harvest financed the family's first car, a Model T Ford. Clara also worked in the Adams Olive Cannery and later at the Monte Vista Hotel, after its conversion to a home for the elderly. She served on the election board and as clerk of the school board, issuing teachers' paychecks. After updating her credential at the University of Southern California, she returned to teaching for two years, in 1919 and 1920, to the same one-room classroom she had left years before. Only this time the old classroom was used as the second classroom in the new two-room Sunland School on Hillrose Street where Clara taught the lower grades.

During heavy rains, water cascaded down Haines

Canyon, formed a river as it crossed Hillrose, and flooded the park. When that happened, both teacher and students enjoyed a surprise holiday because the flood denied anyone access to the school. Sometimes, however, an unexpected storm brought heavy rains while school was in session, trapping the children in the schoolhouse. Crossing the turbulent waters was dangerous, especially for the younger children. Elizabeth remembers such a storm when she was six; the big boys in the upper grades solved the problem by carrying the smaller children across the flooded field to safety. At other times, the children waited for their parents to arrive on horseback to rescue them. The

Looking north on Sherman Grove Avenue circa 1937, one of the few paved streets in Sunland. The Blumfield house is on the right, past the trees.
Photo courtesy of Marshall Murray.

flooding in the park is why Sunland School was eventually moved to the site on Hillrose Street above the water crossing.

With the money she earned teaching, Clara helped finance the construction of three rental cottages on their acre of land. As farmers, they depended on water for a successful crop, especially during the long, hot summer. However, the water supply was not adequate. Without enough rain to fill the watershed during the year, the river simply dried up. Numerous breakdowns with the piping system from Big Tujunga Canyon also interfered with the water flow, and new settlers in the area meant less water for everyone. Sometimes there just wasn't enough water to ensure a healthy crop. During droughts, crops failed for lack of any water at all. Clara and Alfred relied on the rent from the cottages and from other property they bought and leased as basic income.

Clara's outside activities did not interfere with her duties at home. Without today's machines and conveniences, Clara spent hours cleaning, cooking, doing laundry and other household chores, quilting in the front room by the window, and making clothes for Elizabeth's dolls: dresses, aprons, panties, coats, and hats. Farm duties piled on top of house chores. Clara raised chickens; she gathered the eggs, cleaned and candled[19] them in the cellar beneath the house, and then sold them. She hand-churned ice cream and tended a vegetable garden; the first of her sweet corn became a traditional part of the town's Fourth of July festivities.

Alfred and Clara inherited fourteen more acres from Amelia after her death in 1940. When Russ married, they gave their son and his wife Marcie one acre of land, just as Alfred's parents had done for them. Russ built their house at 10822 Sherman Grove, on the hill overlooking the orchards, north of their parents' home. When their twins were born, knowing the difficulty of handling two small babies, Clara traveled a well-worn path from her house to her daughter-in-law's to help with all the chores.

Russ stayed close to home, but Elizabeth did not. While she was attending Occidental College in 1928, Elizabeth became very good friends with Dorothy Foree from San Luis Obispo, California, and Ellice Thompson, from Cashmere, Washington. In the summer of that year, the three girls ventured north to Cashmere to work in the apple orchards. But Elizabeth found more than apples in Washington. There she met Clarence Schell, who followed Elizabeth home after the harvest. He worked in a fruit warehouse in San Fernando until he could convince the twenty-year-old Elizabeth to marry him. They married on Valentine's Day in 1929 and returned to Cashmere, Washington, later that month.

Elizabeth Blumfield and Clarence Schell at Lancasters Lake
just prior to their marriage in 1929.
Photo courtesy of A. Elizabeth Schell.

The distance and the difficulty of travel did not deter Clara from helping Elizabeth when her daughter gave birth to her own four children. Clara traveled all the way to Washington State to welcome each new grandchild.

Pioneer families worked long and hard to transform the land. In working side by side, they developed a closeness that modern technology has eroded. Thinking fondly of an era when families spent more time together, Elizabeth recalls her childhood Christmases when they strung popcorn and made colored paper chains to decorate

Alfred Blumfield (left) with Russ and Elizabeth in the foreground, unidentified man (center), and Mrs. and Mrs. Leonard McVine (right), other early settlers in Monte Vista, enjoying a bit of free time hunting and camping in Little Tujunga Canyon. Photo courtesy of A. Elizabeth Schell.

the tree. "We also put lighted candles on the tree, though I definitely frown on the practice today."[20]

They also shared their leisure time with neighbors, whether for picnics in the park on a Sunday afternoon, celebrations of holidays and weddings, or by enjoying outdoor life in the nearby Big and Little Tujunga Canyons. Early Sunland hotels thrived on visitors from Los Angeles who came to the 'country' for hunting and hiking in the canyons. Locals, too, took advantage of the bounty at their back door both for relaxation and to supply meat for their tables.

On June 26, 1956, Clara and Alfred celebrated their golden wedding anniversary. The young woman who had nervously descended from the train so many years ago had stepped into the town's history. Clara died less than a year later, and Alfred died in 1962.

#####

Map of Sunland Families: Where They Lived

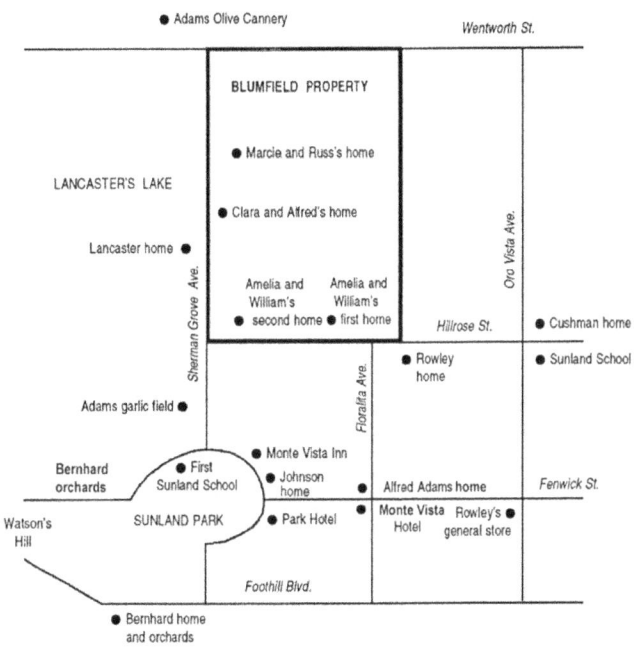

Footnotes

[1] Monte Vista is listed in some history books as a "ghost town" because it failed to develop during the Land Boom of the 1880s. See *Hotels for the Hopeful*, Volume 1 of *The Early History of Sunland, California.*

[2] See *Hotels for the Hopeful.*

[3] Amelia Adams Blumfield: born June 1, 1845 – died March 1940.

[4] William Blumfield: born July 31, 1844, - died July 1927.

[5] Her youngest brother Alfred Adams Sr. lived in Sunland. His son Alfred Jr. established the Adams Olive Cannery.

[6] Her daughter Amelia B. (Millie) Blumfield married Frank Tench. Their son, George Tench, was the first to meet Parson Wornum. See *The Parson and His Cemetery*, Volume 3 of *The Early History of Sunland, California.*

[7] The trunk still remains in the family as a treasured heirloom.

[8] See *From Crackers to Coal Oil*, Volume 4 of *The Early History of Sunland, California.*

[9] Hartranft, M.V., *The Western Empire Land-Banking and Home Securing Plan*, Los Angeles, CA: The Fruit World

Publishing Co., January 1911, p. 21.

[10] The first house was probably near Russett Avenue, although the street didn't exist then.

[11] Their closest neighbors were the Rowleys who lived on Hillrose between Floralita and Oro Vista.

[12] The hill by the 210 Freeway and Foothill Boulevard in Sunland.

[13] Clara Marie Freeman Blumfield: born March 9, 1883 – died April 6, 1957.

[14] The school was located approximately where the baseball fields were later built.

[15] A picture of the first schoolhouse in Sunland Park is found in *From Crackers to Coal Oil*, Volume 4 of *The Early History of Sunland, California*.

[16] Alfred Tunstill Blumfield: born October 5, 1878 – died February 25, 1962.

[17] William Russell Blumfield: born April 16, 1906 – died June 3, 1983. A. (Alma) Elizabeth Blumfield Schell: born May 2, 1908 – still living as of this writing in 2001.

[18] Blumfield, William Russell. Personal interview by Viola L. Carlson, February 19, 1983.

[19] Clara examined the eggs for freshness by holding them up to a bright light.

[20] Schell, A. Elizabeth, *Early Memories of My Childhood*, July 24, 1983.

Bibliography

"Amelia Blumfield, Sunland Pioneer Called by Death." *The Record Ledger*, March 21, 1940.

Blumfield, William Russell. Personal interview by Viola L. Carlson, February 19, 1983.

"Blumfields Have Resided in Same Home on Sherman Grove Since 1906 Marriage." *The Record Ledger*, Historical & Progress Edition. May 21, 1953,

"First Sunland School Founded About 1898 in 1-Room Building." *The Record Ledger*, Historical & Progress Edition, May 21, 1953.

"Golden Wedding." *Tri-City Progress,* September 17, 1915.

Hartranft, M.V., *The Western Empire Land-Banking and Home Securing Plan*, Los Angeles, CA: The Fruit World Publishing Co., January 1911.

"Pioneer Sunland Teacher Dies at Glendale Hospital." *The Record Ledger*, April 11, 1957.

Schell, A. Elizabeth Blumfield. *Early Memories of My Childhood*. July 24, 1983.

Schell, A. Elizabeth Blumfield. Letter to the Board of Sunland-Tujunga Little Landers Historical Society. June 7, 1994.

Schell, A. Elizabeth Blumfield. Letters to Mary Lee Tiernan. 1999-2001.

Schell, A. Elizabeth Blumfield. *Memories of the Past.*

Schell, A. Elizabeth Blumfield. *Random Ramblings: The Memoirs of A. Elizabeth Blumfield Schell.* Cashmere, Washington, July 1990.

Schell, A. Elizabeth Blumfield. *Trips to California.* 2000.

"Sunland First Developed in Big 1887 Land Boom." *The Record Ledger*, September 12, 1968.

"To Move House Out of Oak Tree's Way." *The Record Ledger*, May 3, 1923.

"Where's Monte(a) Vista?" *The Glendale NewsPress,* April 4, 1968.

The Early History of Sunland, California

8 Volume Series
Also available as ebooks

Vol. 1 *Hotels for the Hopeful* Land promoters of the 1880s promised a perfect life of health, wealth, and pleasure. Although their promises fell short of reality, the village did grow and prosper in the hands of farmers.

Vol. 2 *The Roscoe Robbers and the Sensational Train Robbery of 1894* Two robbers posed as passengers to flag down the train. When the engineer recognized danger, he opened the throttle and sped past. The bandits threw the spur switch, and the train careened full speed off the tracks.

Vol. 3 *The Parson and His Cemetery* Parson Wornum was so loved that when he died, the whole village attended his funeral. Years of neglect of his cemetery spelled disaster in 1978 when heavy rains tore open graves and washed bodies down the hillside.

Vol. 4 *From Crackers to Coal Oil* When a student pulled out his gun and laid it on his desk, the tiny one-room school found itself needing a new teacher. That brought Virginia Newcomb, a romance, and a new family that helped to develop the town, leaving behind a detailed account of pioneer life in a small village.

Vol. 5 *He Never Came Home* Joe Ardizzone, a local grape-grower, doubled as a hit-man for the Mafia. During Prohibition, Joe's bootlegging activities caught him in the middle of in-house quarreling. In 1931, he left on a short trip and disappeared into the pages of history.

Vol. 6 *Lancasters Lake* When Edgar Lancaster dredged the swamp on his land, he created a lake which became a treasured landmark. For 25 years, visitors flocked to its cool shores, and Hollywood used the lake as a set location for some of its early movies.

Vol. 7 *Living in Big Tujunga Canyon* Early settlers, like the Johnson family, found their way into the canyon, a dense woodland bristling with wildlife. 50 years later, the Webber family faced the wrath of the river now winding down a denuded mountainside.

Vol. 8 *From Whence They Came* The Land Boom of the 1880s brought immigrants from around the world. Two generations of Blumfields survived the difficulties of farming and water shortages through industry and imagination.

www.ingramcontent.com/pod-product-compliance
Lightning Source LLC
Chambersburg PA
CBHW061348040426
42444CB00011B/3149